Sniff and

By Liza Charlesworth

ISBN: 978-1-339-02669-5

Art Director: Tannaz Fassihi; Designer: Tanya Chernyak
Photos © Getty Images and Shutterstock.com.
Copyright © Liza Charlesworth. All rights reserved. Published by Scholastic Inc.

3 4 5 6 7 8 9 10   68   32 31 30 29 28 27 26 25 24

Printed in Jiaxing, China. First printing, August 2023.

SCHOLASTIC

Sniff, sniff, sniff!
A nose helps us
to smell.

A nose can sniff a lot!
It can smell a plant.
It can smell a skunk.

A nose can tell us
about a snack.

It can tell us
about a sock.

A smell can be small and good.
Snip, snip, snip!

A smell can be big and bad.
Yuck, yuck, ick!

A dog has a nose to smell.

A cat and a fox do as well.

Sniff, sniff, sniff!
It is fun to smell.
A nose is a big help!